THE LIBRARY

GUITAR CLASSICS

COMPILED AND ARRANGED BY JERRY WILLARD

ORDER NO. AM 943261
US INTERNATIONAL STANDARD BOOK NUMBER: 0.8256.1620.4
UK INTERNATIONAL STANDARD BOOK NUMBER: 0.7119.6490.4

EXCLUSIVE DISTRIBUTORS:
MUSIC SALES CORPORATION
257 PARK AVENUE SOUTH, NEW YORK, NY 10010 USA
MUSIC SALES LIMITED
8/9 FRITH STREET, LONDON W1V 5TZ ENGLAND
MUSIC SALES PTY. LIMITED
120 ROTHSCHILD STREET, ROSEBERY, SYDNEY, NSW 2018, AUSTRALIA

PRINTED IN THE UNITED STATES OF AMERICA BY
VICKS LITHOGRAPH AND PRINTING CORPORATION

AMSCO PUBLICATIONS
NEW YORK/LONDON/PARIS/SYDNEY

Pavana No. 4

Luis Milan
1500 – 1561

Pavana No. 5

Luis Milan

Pavana No. 6

Luis Milan

Balleto

Jean-Baptiste Besard
c. 1567 – c. 1617

Branle

Jean-Baptiste Besard

The Frog Galliard

John Dowland
1562 – 1626

Lachrimae Pavan

John Dowland

Melancholy Galliard

John Dowland

Come Away

John Dowland

Can She Excuse
(Earl of Essex's Galliard)

John Dowland

Mrs. Nichol's Almain

John Dowland

John Dowland's Galliard

John Dowland

Mrs. Winter's Jump

John Dowland

Orlando Sleepeth

John Dowland

La Cavalleria de Napoles

Gaspar Sanz
1640 – 1710

Folias

Gaspar Sanz

Prelude and Allegro

Santiago de Murcia
1685? – 1732?

Suite in D Minor

Robert de Visee
1660 – 1720

Prelude

Allemande

23

Courante

24

Sarabande

Gavotte

Menuet (Rondeau)

26

Menuet

Bouree

Gigue

Sarabande with Variations

George Frideric Handel
1685 – 1759

Sonata

Mateo Albéniz
c. 1755 – 1831

⑥ = D

Allegro

Sonata
Longo 352

Domenico Scarlatti
1685 – 1757

Sonata
Longo 263

Domenico Scarlatti

Capricio

Sylvius Leopold Weiss
1686 – 1750

Minuet

Sylvius Leopold Weiss

D.C. al Fine

Fuge in A Minor
BWV 1000

Johann Sebastian Bach
1685 – 1750

44

Suite IV
BWV 1006a

Johann Sebastian Bach

Prelude

Loure

Gavotte en rondeau

Menuet I

Menuet II

Da Capo Menuet I (al 𝄐)

58

Bouree

Gigue

Allegretto

Ferdinando Carulli
1770 – 1841

Ten Preludes

Ferdinando Carulli

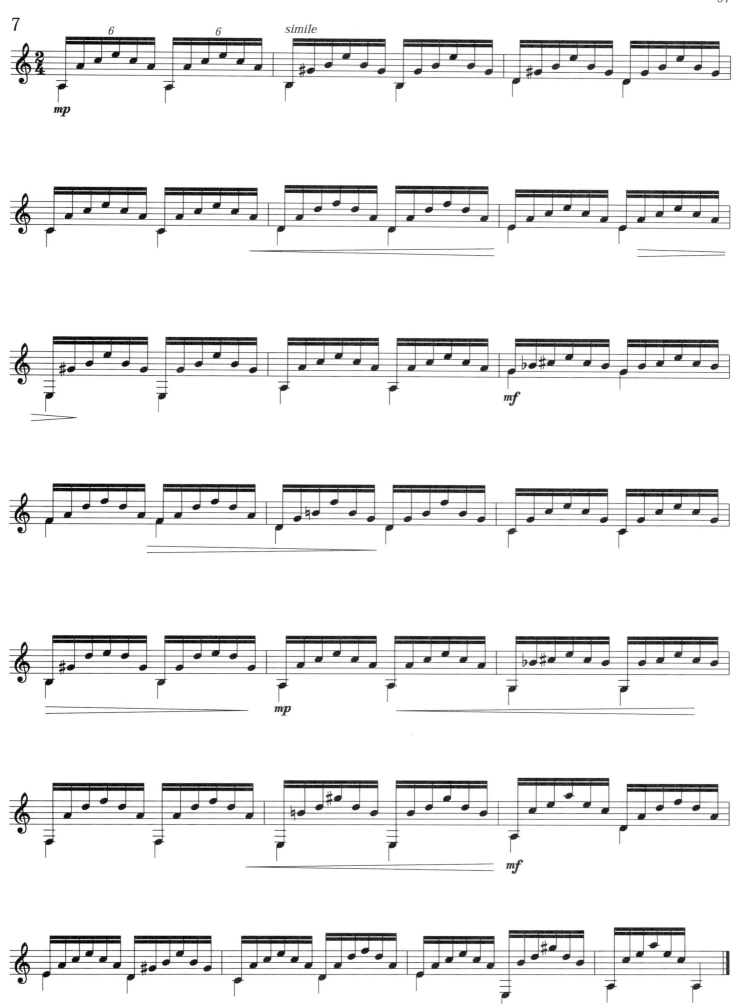

8

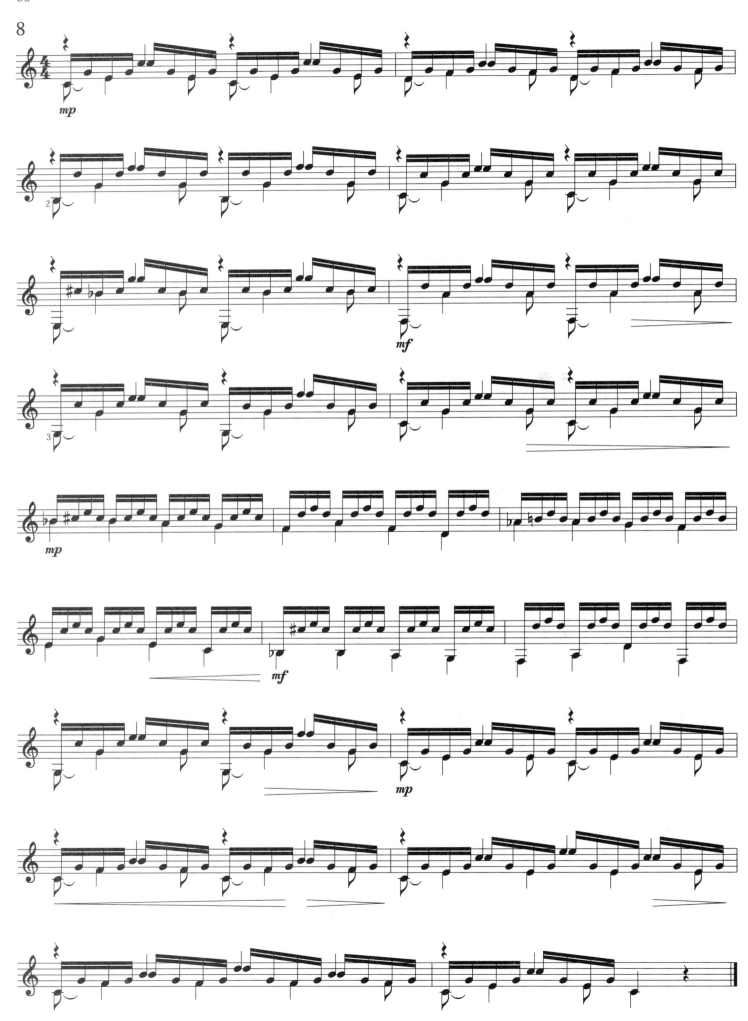

10

Duet in E Minor

Ferdinando Carulli

D.C. al Fine

Rondo

Allegretto con poco moto

Duet in D

I

Ferdinando Carulli

Largo

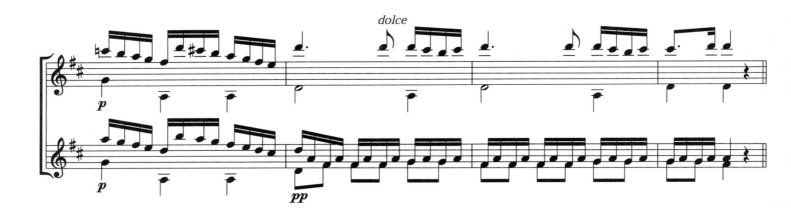

Rondo

Allegretto

Minore

Allegretto

Fernando Sor
1778 – 1839

Allegro

Fernando Sor

Andantino

Fernando Sor

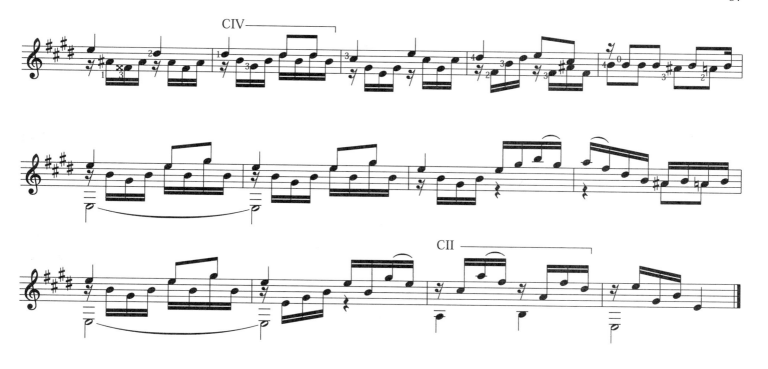

Giocoso

Mauro Giuliani
1781 – 1828

Scherzo, Allegro vivace

Trio

D.C. al Fine

L'Allegria

Mauro Giuliani

Morceaux Caractéristiques

Mauro Giuliani

La Penser

Le Lis

Le Jasmin

La Rose

L' Amoroso

Minore

Maggiore

Rossiniane

Introduzione

Mauro Giuliani

*in original:

Eroica Sonata

Mauro Giuliani

Study No. 1

Matteo Carcassi
1792 – 1853

Study No. 6

Matteo Carcassi

Study No. 11

Matteo Carcassi

Study No. 16

Matteo Carcassi

Study No. 18

Matteo Carcassi

Study No. 23

Matteo Carcassi

D.C. al Fine

Twenty-one Lessons

Dionisio Aguado
1784 – 1849

1

11

12 **Allegro moderato**

13

14

19

21

Study in E Minor

Dionisio Aguado

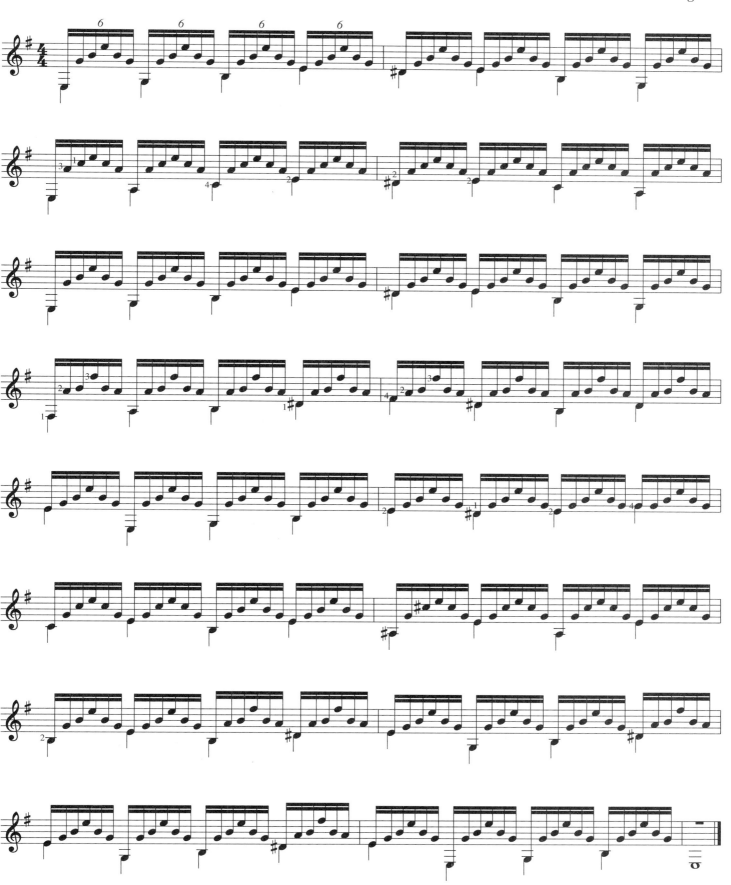

Study in G

Dionisio Aguado

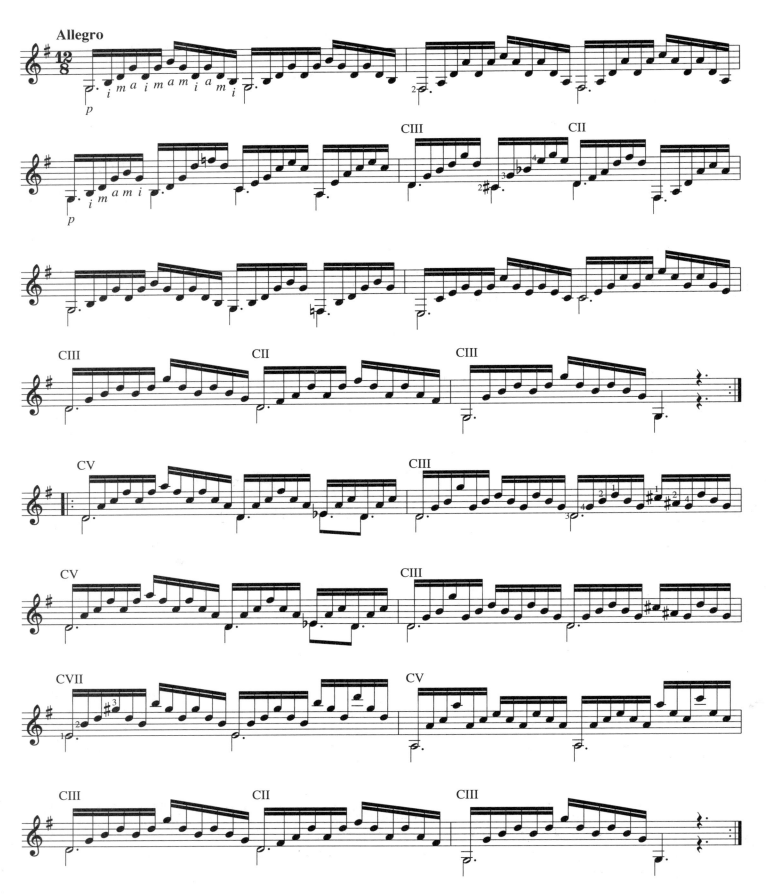

Le Fandango

Dionisio Aguado

Allegro vivace

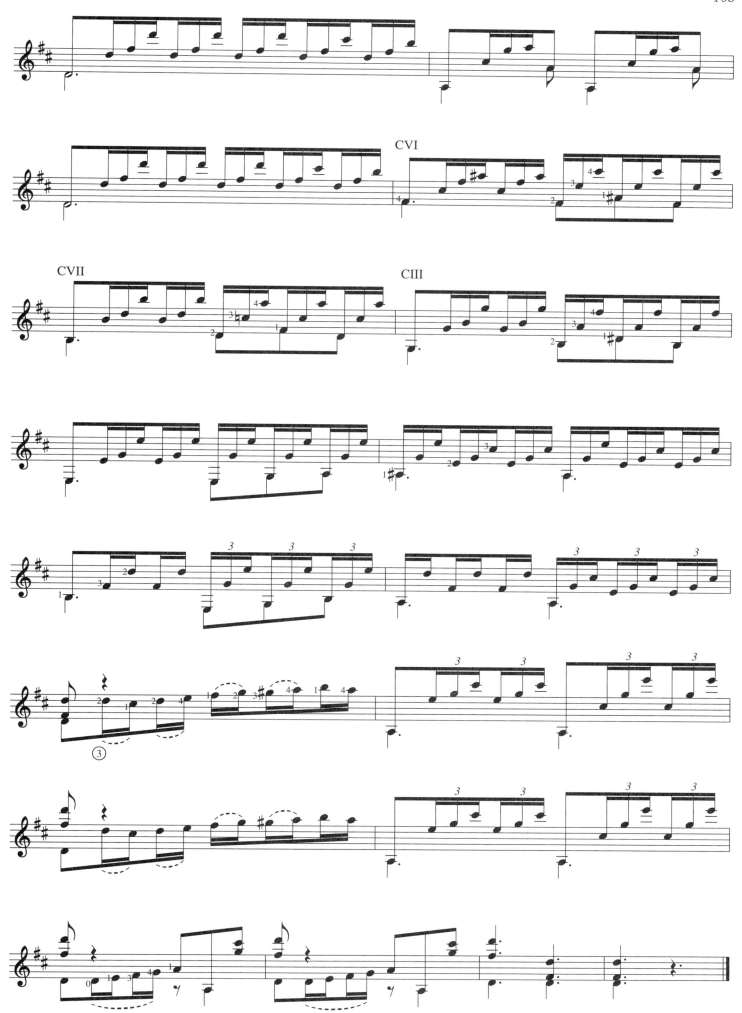

Rondo in A Minor

Dionisio Aguado

Grand Sonata

Niccolò Paganini
1782 – 1840

1. Allegro Risoluto

2. Romanze

Più tosto largo. Amorosamente

dolce

3. Andantino variato

Var. II

Var. III

Var. IV

Var. V

Var. VI

morendo

Sonata No. 1

Niccolò Paganini

Study in E Minor

Napoleon Coste
1806 – 1883

Rondo

Napoleon Coste

Study in A

Napoleon Coste

Las Dos Hermanitas

Francisco Tárrega
1852 – 1909

Trio

Vals

Francisco Tárrega

Pavana

Allegretto

Francisco Tárrega

Sueño
Mazurka

Francisco Tárrega

Gran Vals

Francisco Tárrega

Danza Mora

Francisco Tárrega

Al eminente maestro D. Tomás Breton

Capricho Árabe

Serenata

Fransisco Tárrega

poco cresc.

accel.

Adelita
Mazurka

Francisco Tárrega

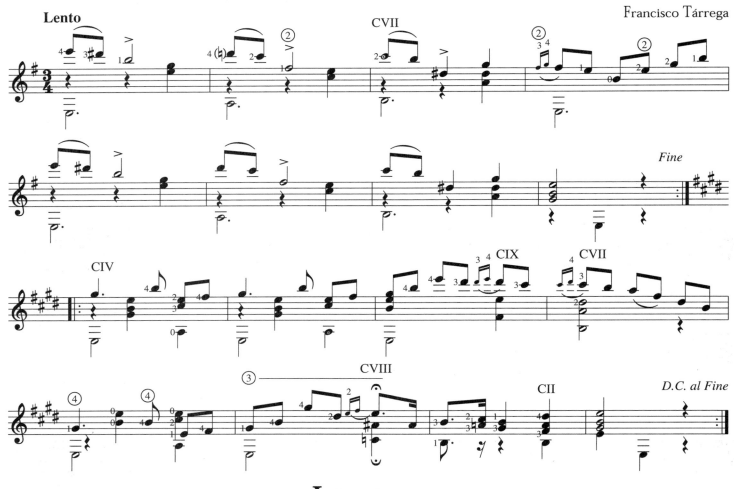

Lágrima

Francisco Tárrega

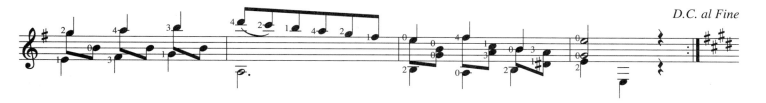

D.C. al Fine

Little Piece

Robert Schumann
1810 – 1856

Allegro moderato

Little Song

Robert Schumann

Melody

Robert Schumann

La Maja de Goya

Enrique Granados
1867 – 1916

Dedicatoria

Enrique Granados

Spanish Dance No. 2

Oriental

Enrique Granados

Lento assai

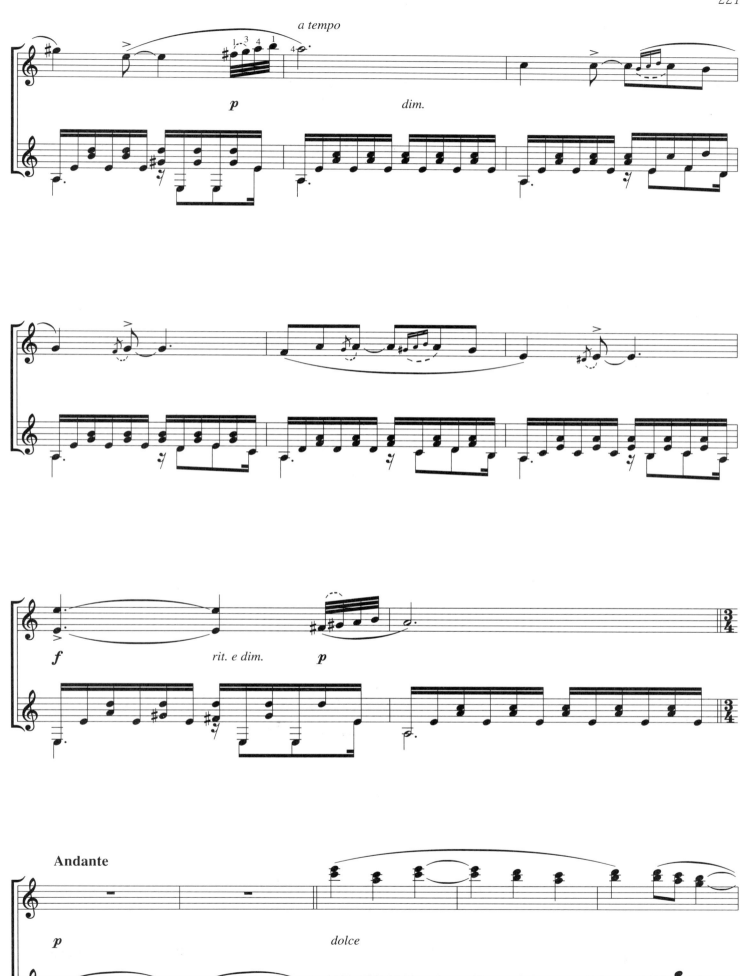

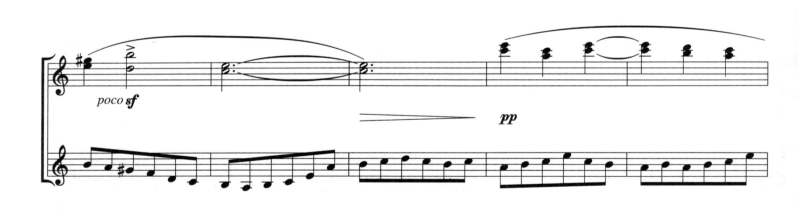

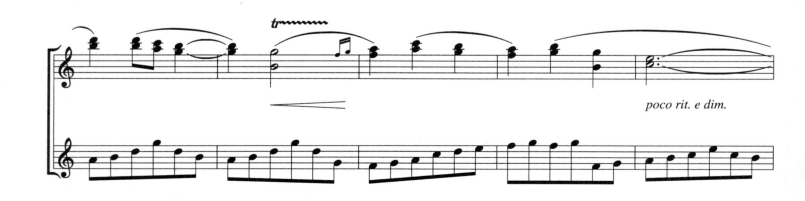

Valses Poeticos

Enrique Granados

Valse No. 1

Valse No. 2

Tempo de Valse noble

Valse No. 3

Valse No. 4

Valse No. 5

Valse No. 6

Valse No. 7

Valse No. 1
(reprise)

Mallorca
(Barcarola)

Isaac Albéniz
1860 – 1909